W9-AWF-134

Time-to-Discover SCHOLASTIC READERS

Polar Animal Babies

Melvin and Gilda Berger

SCHOLASTIC INC.
New York Toronto London Auckland Sydney
Mexico City New Delhi Hong Kong Buenos Aires

Photographs: Cover: Daniel J. Cox/Getty Images;
p. 1: Tom Murphy/WWI/Peter Arnold, Inc.; p. 3: Frans Lanting/Minden Pictures;
p. 4: Norbert Rosing/Getty Images; p. 5: Daniel J. Cox/Getty Images;
p. 6: Amos Nachoum/Corbis; p. 7: Yves Lefevre/Peter Arnold, Inc.;
p. 8: Bill Curtsinger/National Geographic Society; p. 9: Michio Hoshino/Minden Pictures;
p. 10: Daniel J. Cox/Natural Exposures; p. 11: Norbert Rosing/Getty Images;
p. 12: Michio Hoshino/Minden Pictures; p. 13: Michio Hoshino/Minden Pictures;
p. 14: Tui De Roy/Minden Pictures; p. 15: Kim Heacox/Accent Alaska;
p. 16: Beth Davidow/Getty Images.

Photo Research: Dwayne Howard

No part of this publication may be reproduced, stored in a retrieval system,
or transmitted in any form or by any means, electronic, mechanical,
photocopying, recording, or otherwise, without written permission
of the publisher. For information regarding permission,
write to Scholastic Inc., Attention: Permissions Department,
557 Broadway, New York, NY 10012.

ISBN 0-439-81533-9

Text copyright © 2006 by Melvin and Gilda Berger
All rights reserved. Published by Scholastic Inc.
SCHOLASTIC, SCHOLASTIC TIME-TO-DISCOVER READERS, and associated logos are
trademarks and/or registered trademarks of Scholastic Inc.

12 11 10 9 8 7 6 5 4 3 2 1   6 7 8 9 10 11/0

Printed in the U.S.A.
First printing, January 2006

Polar animal babies look like their moms and dads.

Polar bears are born in snow den

Fun Fact

Mother and cubs stay together for about two years.

Baby polar bears are called cubs.

Whales are born in the ocean.

Baby whales are called calves.

Seals are born in snow dens.

Fun Fact

Seal pups feed on their mother's milk.

Baby seals are called pups.

Fun Fact

Both parents help feed the cub.

Arctic foxes are born in underground dens.

Baby foxes are called cubs.

Fun Fact

The mother feeds chicks of all ages in the same nest.

Snowy owls hatch from eggs.

Baby snowy owls
are called chicks.

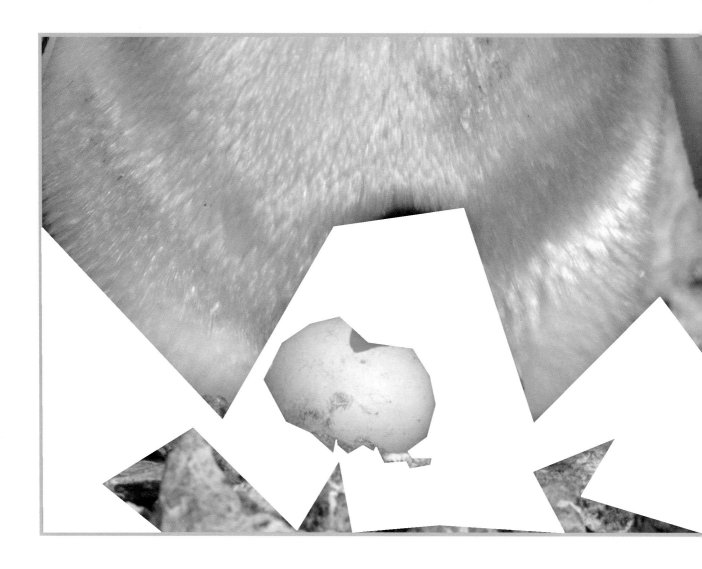

Penguins hatch from eggs.

Baby penguins are called chicks.

Polar animal babies grow up fast.